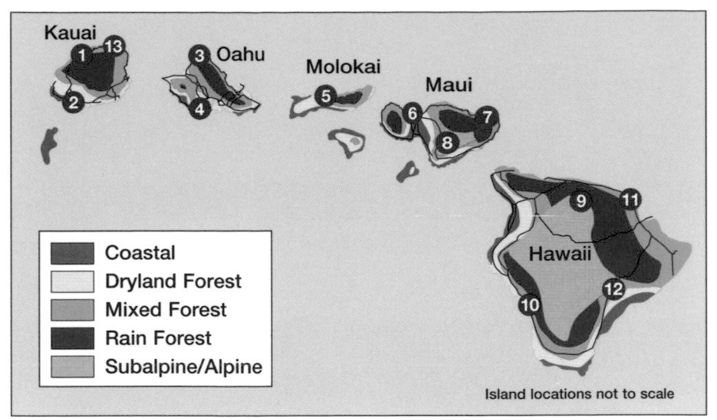

1. Limahuli Gardens & Preserve
2. Allerton/McBryde Gardens
3. Waimea Valley Audubon Center
4. Foster Botanical Garden
5. Kalaupapa National Historical Park
6. Maui Nui Botanical Gardens
7. Kahanu Garden
8. Kula Botanical Garden
9. Hakalau Forest National Wildlife Refuge
10. Kealakekua Bay State Historical Park
11. Hawaii Tropical Botanical Garden
12. Hawaii Volcanoes National Park
13. Na ‘Āina Kai Botanical Gardens

Hawaii is home to a vast diversity of plants including over 1,000 native and hundreds of introduced species. The introduced species were brought by settlers for food, ornament and medicine; many have since escaped to become naturalized on the islands. The first settlers, and the first infusion of non-native plants, occurred when the Polynesians began arriving from the Marquesas about 500 A.D. The second wave of non-native plants began arriving from around the world following Captain Cook's discovery of the islands in 1778.

Today, many of Hawaii's native lands have been drastically altered by introduced species to the point that, in many areas, the foreign species dominate the landscape. In order to separate native from introduced species, the plants in this guide are coded as:

Native species Introduced from Polynesia Introduced after 1778

Measurements denote the height of plants unless otherwise indicated. Illustrations are not to scale.

Made in the USA

Waterford Press publishes reference guides that introduce readers to nature observation, outdoor recreation and survival skills. Product information is featured on the website: **www.waterfordpress.com**

To order or for information on custom published products please call 800-434-2555 or email orderdesk@waterfordpress.com. For permissions or to share comments email editor@waterfordpress.com.

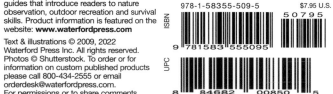

ISBN 978-1-58355-509-5 $7.95 U.S.
9 781583 555095 50795
UPC 8 84682 00850 5
10 9 8 7 6 5 4 3 2 1 2204706

HAWAII TREES & WILDFLOWERS – A Folding Pocket Guide to Familiar Plants

Kavanagh/Leung

A POCKET NATURALIST® GUIDE

HAWAII
TREES & WILDFLOWERS

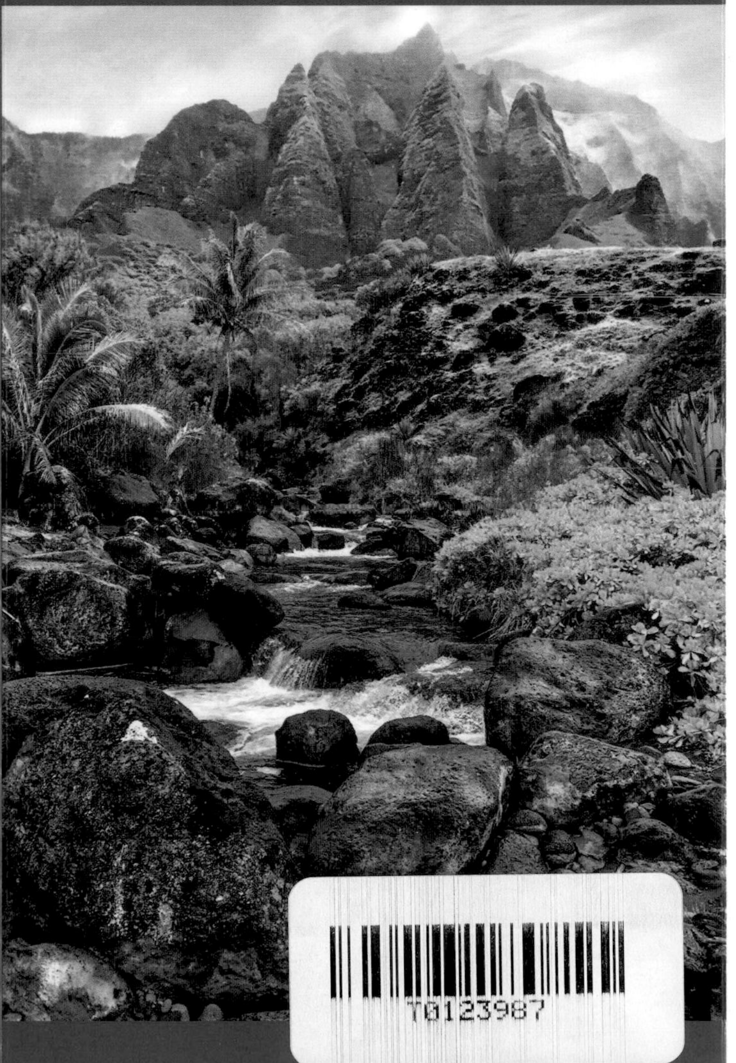

A Folding Pocket Guide to Familiar Plants

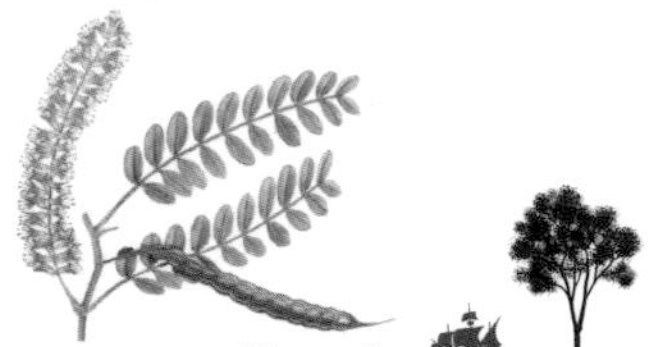

Algaroba
Prosopis pallida To 60 ft. (18 m)
Thorny tree has fern-like leaves. Flowers bloom in long spikes and are succeeded by yellow seed pods. The wood is used for charcoal, the beans for livestock food. Native to South America.

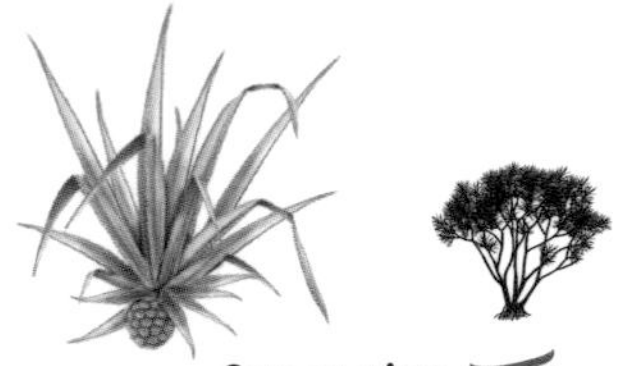

Screw-pine
Pandanus tectorius To 30 ft. (9 m)
Palm-like tree has numerous prop roots around its base. Long narrow leaves are arranged in screw-like spirals at the ends of branches. Fruit looks like a pineapple from a distance.

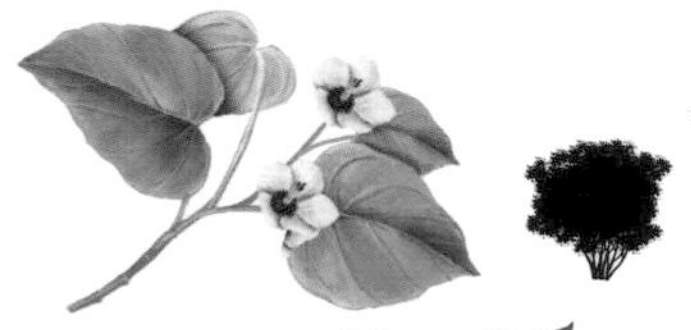

Sea Hibiscus
Hibiscus tiliaceus To 33 ft. (10 m)
Each 3 in./8 cm flower lasts a single day, blooming yellow in the morning and turning to red-orange before dropping off. Forms dense stands in river valleys and along lowland streams.

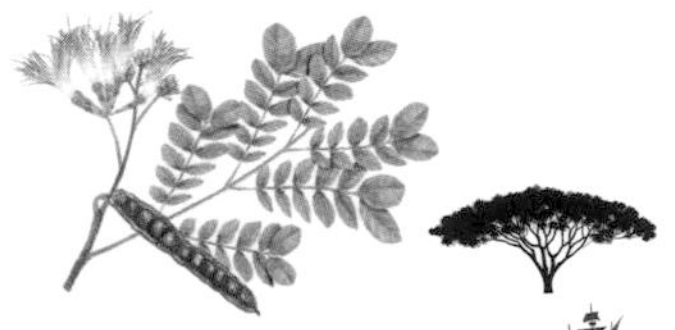

Monkeypod Tree
Samanea saman To 75 ft. (23 m)
Note symmetrical, umbrella-shaped profile. Fern-like leaves fall off the tree in early spring. Pink puffy flowers are succeeded by long seed pods (to 8 in./20 cm) in autumn. Native to South America.

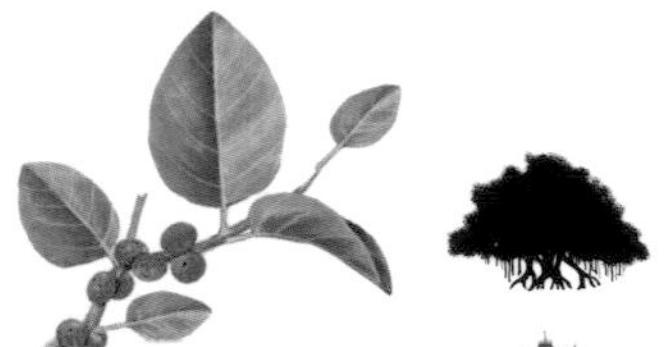

Indian Banyan
Ficus benghalensis To 100 ft. (30 m)
Distinctive tree puts down aerial roots that create a maze of trunks. Large trees can cover an acre.

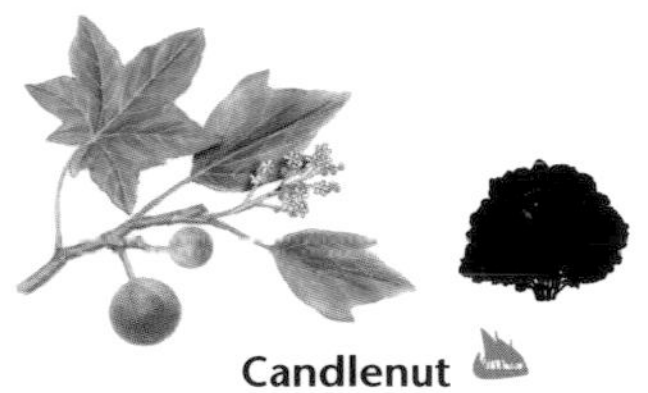

Candlenut
Aleurites moluccana To 80 ft. (24 m)
Maple-like leaves are covered in white hairs making the foliage appear light green at a distance. Walnut-like fruits are a source of oil which was burned in lamps. The roasted seeds are a favorite snack. **Hawaii's state tree.**

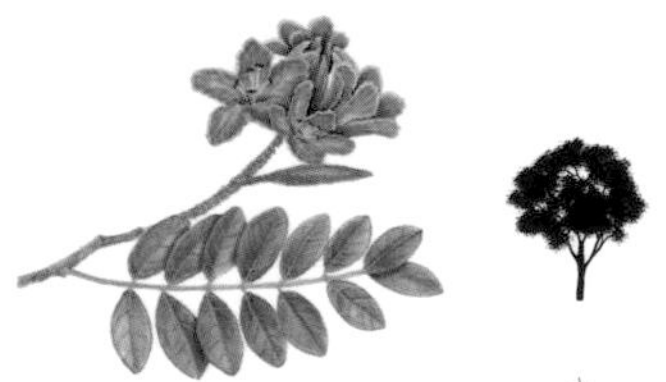

African Tulip Tree
Spathodea campanulata
To 70 ft. (21 m)
Distinguished by its masses of bright orange-red blossoms. An introduced ornamental, it has become fully naturalized and grows in the wild.

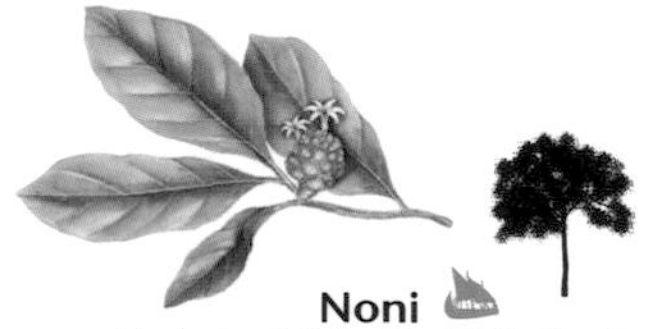

Noni
Morinda citrifolia To 20 ft. (6 m)
Shrub or small tree has large, glossy leaves with prominent yellow veins. White flowers are succeeded by a lumpy, lemon-sized fruit.

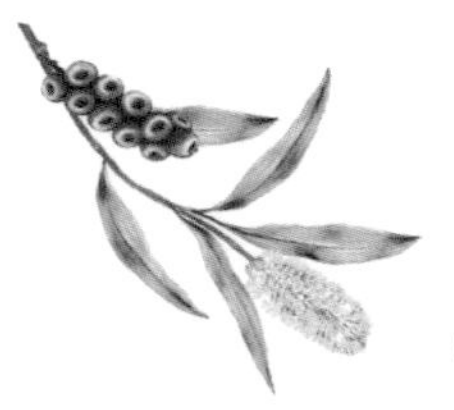

Paperbark (Cajeput) Tree
Melaleuca quinquenervia
To 50 ft. (15 m)
Trunk and branches have shredding bark. Whitish flowers bloom in showy "bottlebrush" clusters and are succeeded by small rounded fruits.

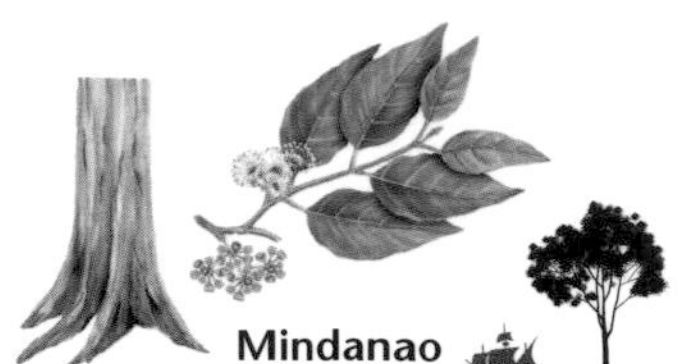

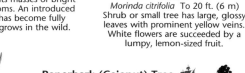

Mindanao Gum
Eucalyptus deglupta To 80 ft. (24 m)
Easily distinguished by its bark which looks as if it has had paint dripped down its sides. A widely planted ornamental native to the Philippines.

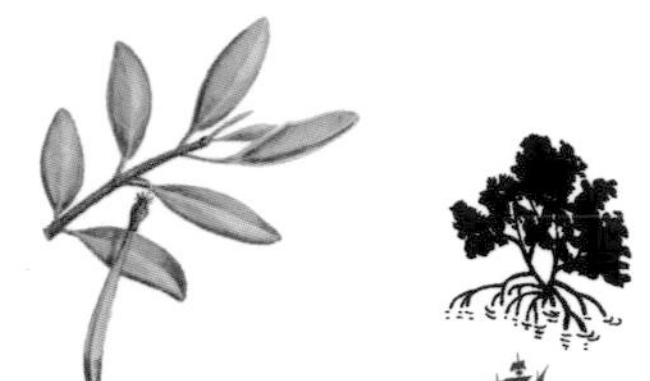

Red Mangrove
Rhizophora mangle To 80 ft. (24 m)
Coastal evergreen tree produces dense tangles of prop roots along shorelines. Has shiny leaves and torpedo-shaped seedlings. Introduced from America to hold the soil along mudflats.

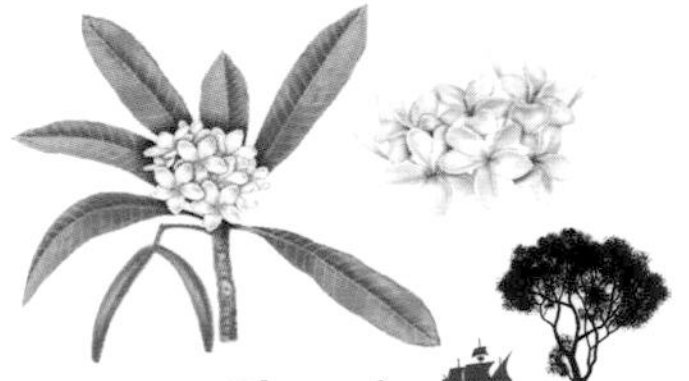

Plumeria
Plumeria spp. To 30 ft. (9 m)
Waxy white, pink or yellow flowers appear in the spring before the leaves. A very common ornamental, the "pua melia" is a popular lei flower. Native to tropical America.

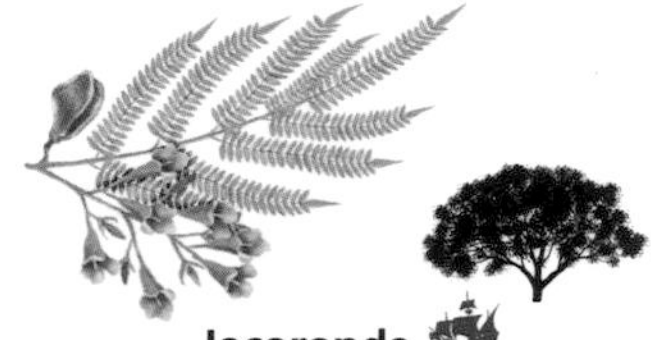

Jacaranda
Jacaranda mimosifolia To 50 ft. (15 m)
Has delicate, fern-like leaves and masses of lavender, bell-shaped flowers. Native to South America.

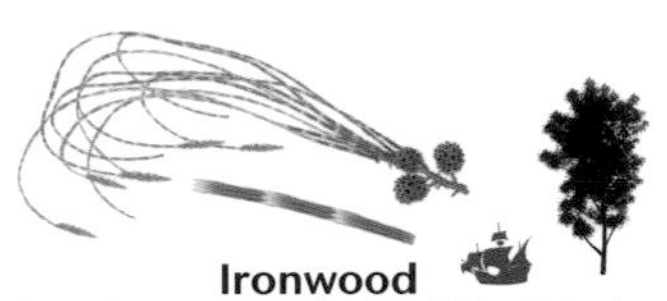

Ironwood
Casuarina equisetifolia To 80 ft. (24 m)
Large tree has long, thin needle-like twigs. Fruits are a hard, brown cone. Grows well in dry areas and is often used for windbreaks along beaches. Native to Australia.

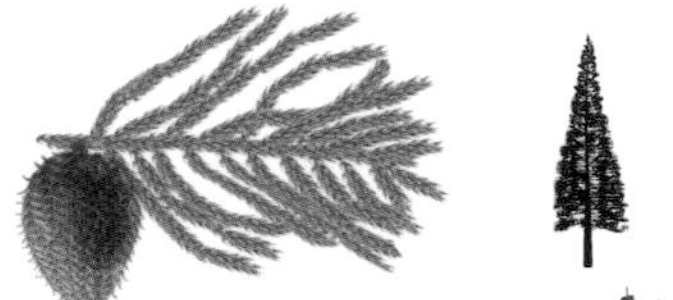

Cook (Columnar) Pine
Araucaria columnaris To 200 ft. (61 m)
Not a true pine, it has small scale-like leaves growing long twigs. Crown grows in many shapes ranging from pyramids to straight columns.

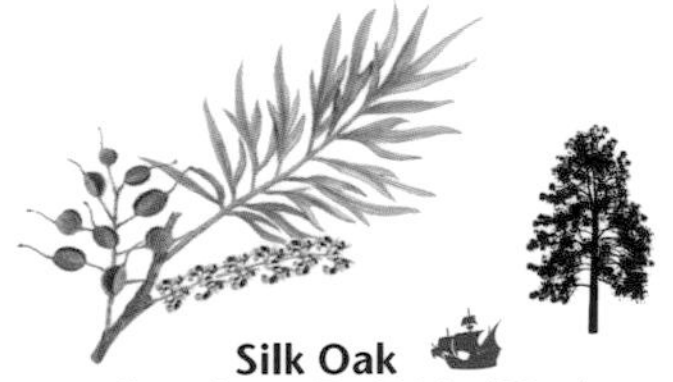

Silk Oak
Grevillea robusta To 100 ft. (30 m)
Has fern-like leaves and masses of orange, fringed blossoms. Named for its wood with a silky, oak-like texture. A widely planted ornamental, it is native to Australia.

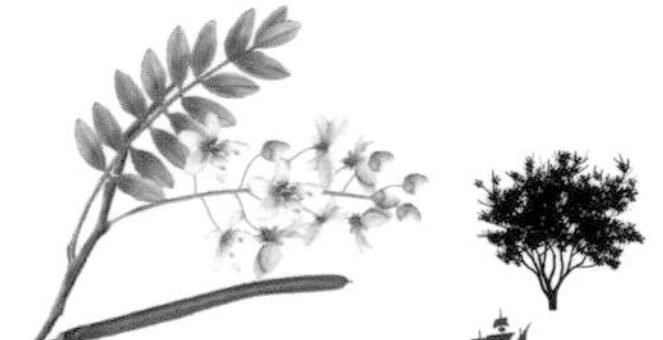

Shower Tree
Cassia spp. To 60 ft. (18 m)
Gorgeous flowering tree has blossoms that may be golden, pink, coral or white. Hybrids of two of these (rainbow shower trees) feature blossoms of mixed colors. Several species were introduced from tropical areas worldwide.

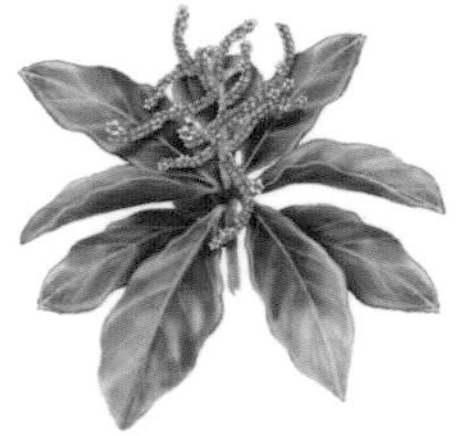

Tree Heliotrope
Tournefortia argentea
To 20 ft. (6 m)
Common beach tree has an umbrella-shaped crown up to 40 ft. (12 m) wide. Flowers and fruits grow in tightly packed, coiled strands. Native to the Indian Ocean area.

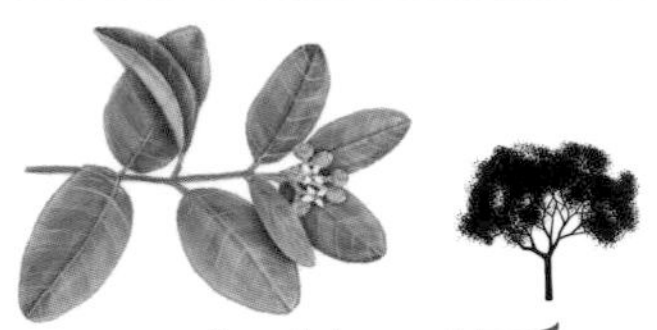

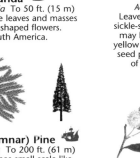

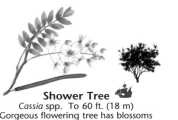

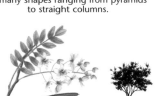

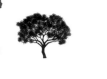

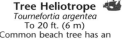

Sandalwood
Santalum spp. To 100 ft. (30 m)
Light green leaves are leathery. Flowers may be yellow, red or greenish. Wood was prized for its fine-grained quality and pleasant aroma. Exporting the wood to China almost wiped out the species in the late 1700s.

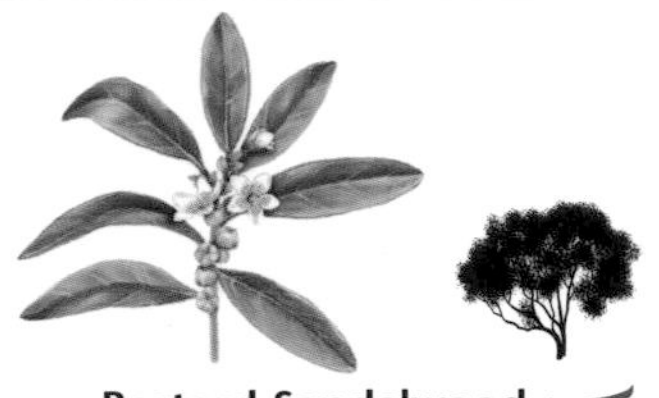

Bastard Sandalwood
Myoporum sandwicense
To 60 ft. (18 m)
Shrub or tree has dark green leaves which often appear twisted. Bell-shaped white to pink flowers are succeeded by waxy fruits. Has qualities like true sandalwood but they are less-pronounced. Grows in association with mamane.

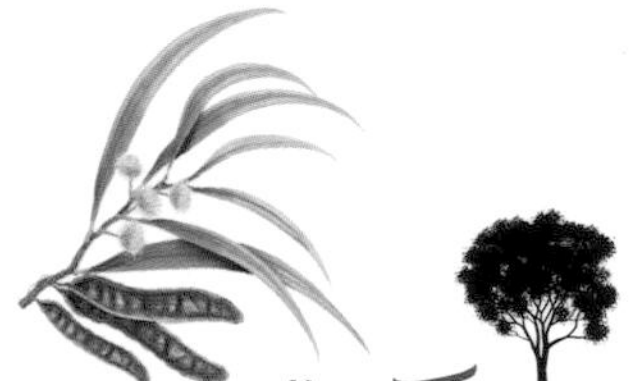

Koa
Acacia koa To 100 ft. (30 m)
Leaves are fern-like when young and sickle-shaped when mature; both types may be found on a single tree. Puffy yellow flowers are succeeded by brown seed pods to 6 in. (15 cm) long. One of Hawaii's largest native trees.

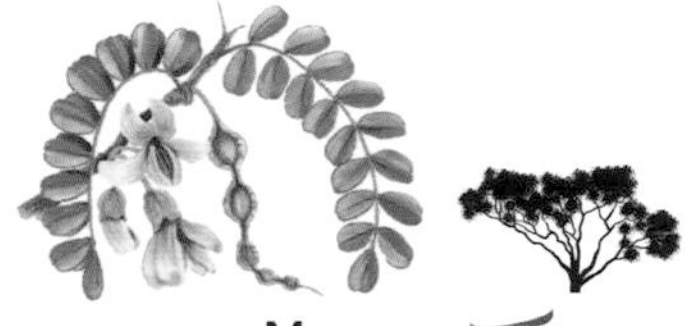

Mamane
Sophora chrysophylla To 45 ft. (13.5 m)
Has down-curving leaves and pea-like yellow flowers. The dominant plant in subalpine areas of east Maui and Hawaii.

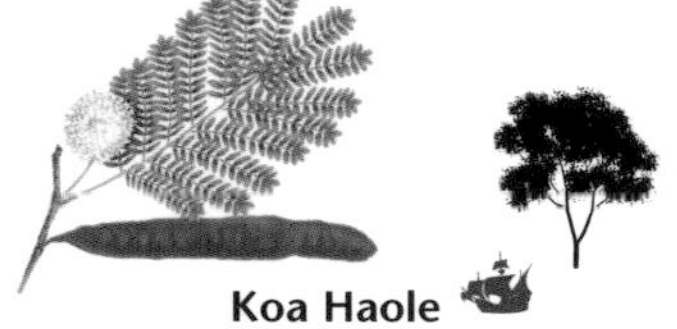

Koa Haole
Leucaena leucocephala To 20 ft. (6 m)
Puffy white flowers are succeeded by long bean pods. Native to tropical America, it was introduced because it grows well in poor soil and feeds livestock. Invasive.

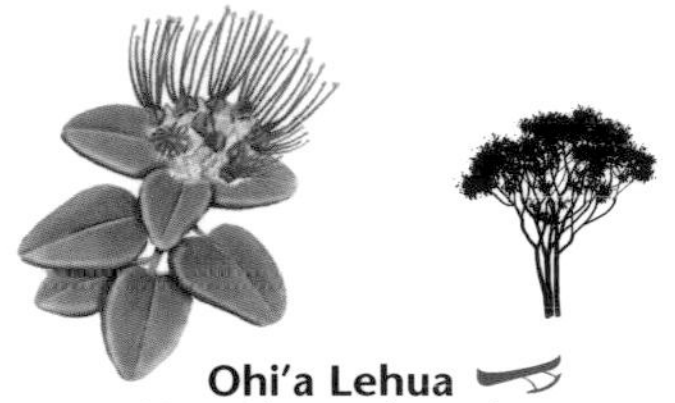

Ohi'a Lehua
Metrosideros polymorpha
To 100 ft. (30 m)
Tree or shrub has distinctive spiky flowers that may be red, pink, yellow or white. The most common native tree, it grows in a variety of habitats.

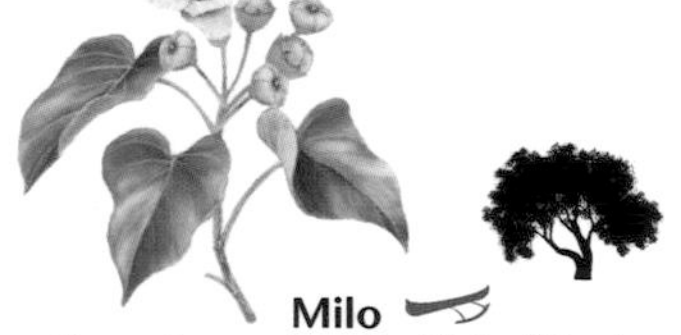

Milo
Thespesia populnea To 30 ft. (10 m)
Erect coastal tree has glossy, heart-shaped leaves. Hibiscus-like yellow flowers have purplish centers. Prized for its wood.

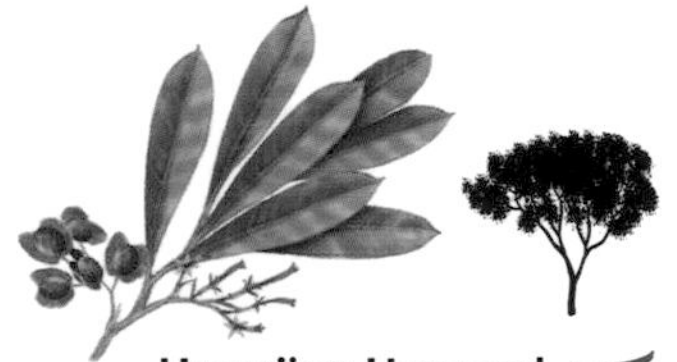

Hawaiian Hopseed
Dodonaea viscosa To 30 ft. (9 m)
Shrub or small tree has papery leaves widest near the tip. Tiny flowers are succeeded by bright red to purple papery, winged lantern-like fruits.

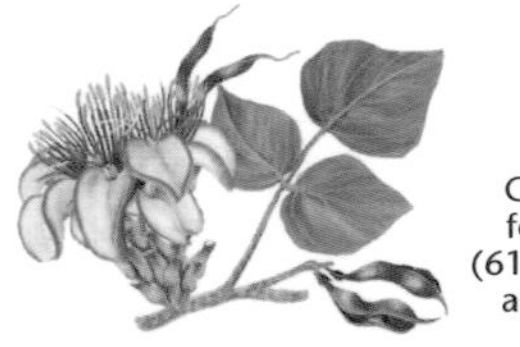

Wiliwili
Erythrina sandwicensis
To 50 ft. (15 m)
Gnarled trees are common in dry forests from sea level to 2,000 ft. (610 m). Leaves drop in summer and are replaced by yellowish flowers.

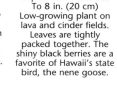

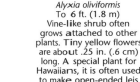

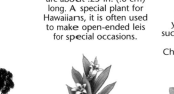

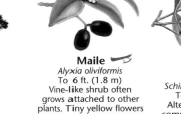

Royal Poinciana
Delonix regia To 40 ft. (12 m)
The tree's brilliant red/orange, scarlet flowers bloom from spring until autumn. Seed pods persist on tree through winter. Native to Madagascar.

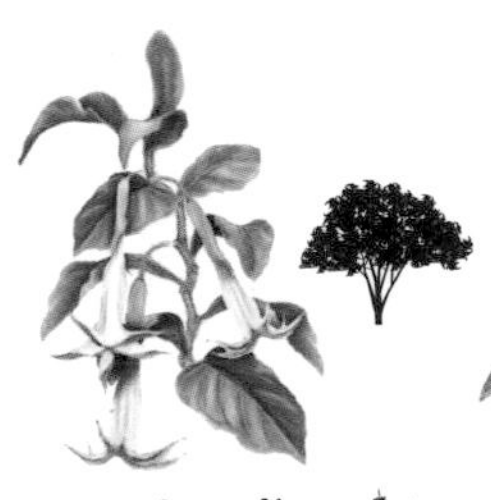

Angel's Trumpet
Datura candida
To 15 ft. (4.5 m)
Small tree has large, hanging trumpet-shaped flowers up to 10 in. (25 cm) long. Native to tropical America.

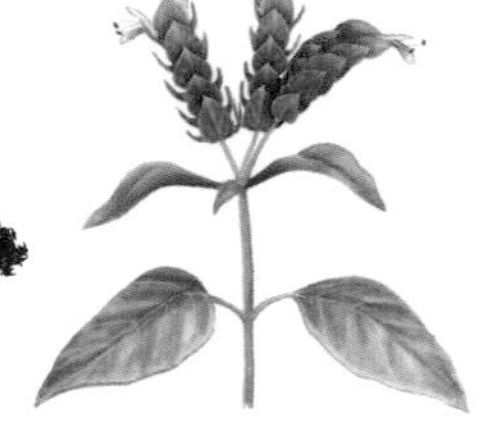

Shrimp Plant
Justica brandegeeana
To 8 ft. (2.4 m)
Weak-stemmed shrub has purplish stems. Whitish flowers bloom in a curving spike between overlapping salmon-colored bracts. Native to Mexico.

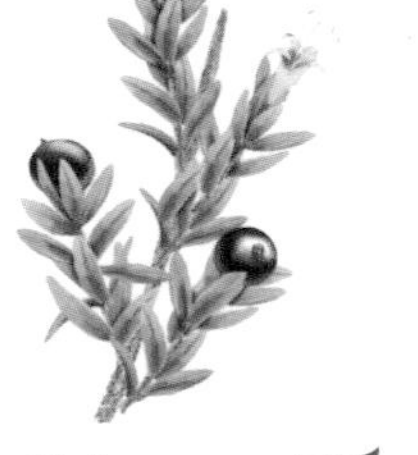

Kukaenene
Coprosma ernodeoides
To 8 in. (20 cm)
Low-growing plant on lava and cinder fields. Leaves are tightly packed together. The shiny black berries are a favorite of Hawaii's state bird, the nene goose.

Maile
Alyxia oliviformis
To 6 ft. (1.8 m)
Vine-like shrub often grows attached to other plants. Tiny yellow flowers are about .25 in. (.6 cm) long. A special plant for Hawaiians, it is often used to make open-ended leis for special occasions.

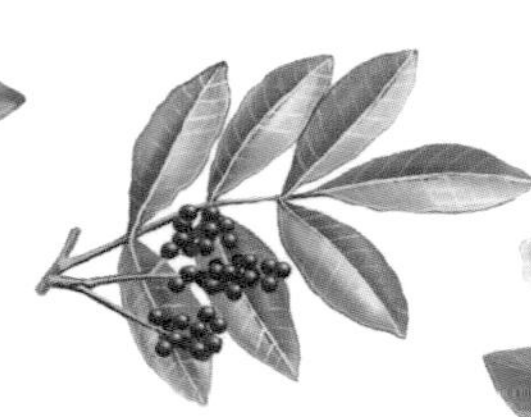

Brazilian Pepper
Schinus terebinthifolius
To 50 ft. (15 m)
Alternate, evergreen compound leaves have up to 40 leaflets. Elongate clusters of yellowish flowers are succeeded by red berries. Known locally as Christmasberry. Invasive.

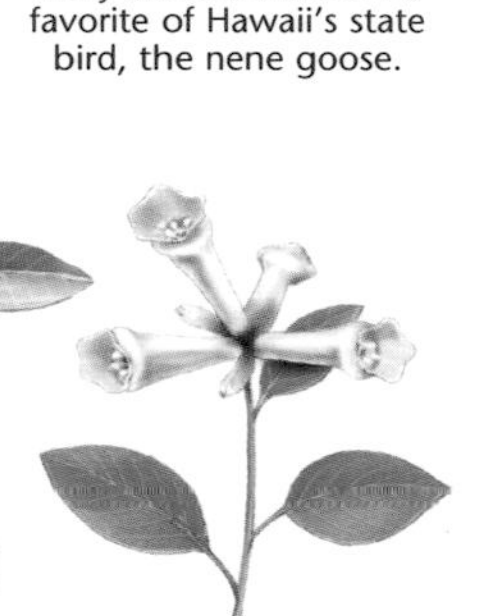

Tree Tobacco
Nicotiana spp.
To 10 ft. (3 m)
Spindly tree or shrub has trumpet-shaped yellow flowers. Invasive.

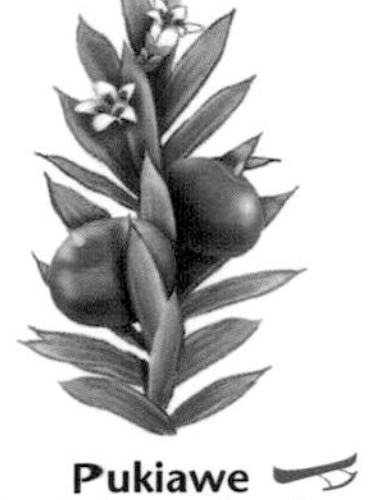

Pukiawe
Styphelia tameiameiae
To 8 in. (20 cm)
Stiff trailside shrub has small oval leaves. Tiny flowers are succeeded by clusters of white to maroon berries to .25 in. (.6 cm) in diameter.

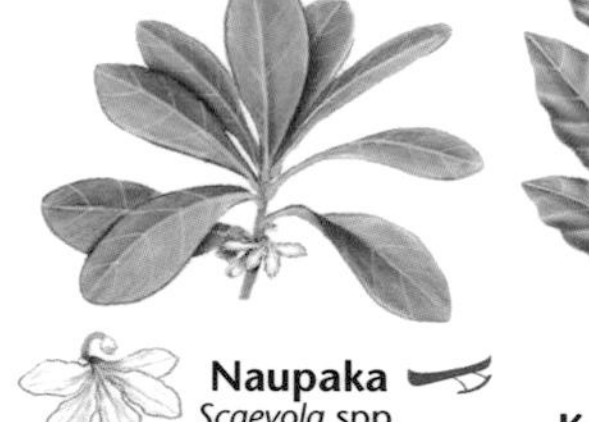

Naupaka
Scaevola spp.
To 3 ft. (90 cm)
Common shrubs have white, yellow or lavender flowers that look as if half is missing. A common landscape plant at resorts.

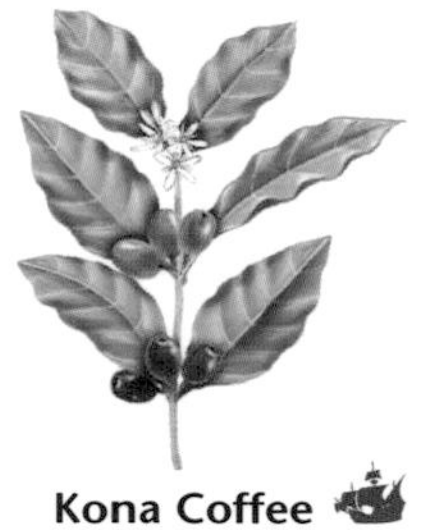

Kona Coffee
Coffee arabica
To 30 ft. (9 m)
Has shiny green leaves. White flowers are succeeded by and berries. Native to tropical Africa.

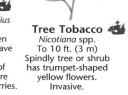

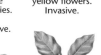

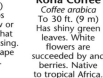

INTRODUCED FOOD PLANTS

Avocado
Persea americana To 40 ft. (12 m)
A common understory tree. Sprays of yellow flowers are succeeded by the familiar lumpy fruits that consist of 30% oil. Native to tropical America.

Macadamia Tree
Macadamia integrifolia
To 65 ft. (20 m)
Small flowers bloom in long clusters and are succeeded by the popular nuts. The nuts ripen year round and are eaten raw and roasted. Native to Australia.

Mango
Mangifera indica To 70 ft. (21 m)
Trees have thick trunks and dense crowns of lance-shaped leaves up to 12 in. (30 cm) long. A valuable source of fruit and wood, it was introduced from India in the early 1800s.

Lychee
Litchi chinensis To 50 ft. (15 m)
Tree is prized for its lumpy red fruits (to 1.5 in./4 cm) which are served fresh or dried. Native to China.

Breadfruit
Artocarpus altilis To 60 ft. (18 m)
Leathery leaves are up to 3 ft. (90 cm) long. Fruits are up to 10 in. (25 cm) in diameter and weigh 10 lbs. (4.5 kg).

Coconut Palm
Cocos nucifera To 100 ft. (30 m)
Arched trunk supports large crown of feathery leaves. Fruit is a fibrous nut to 14 in. (35 cm) long. A valuable source of food and water.

Guava
Psidium guajava To 30 ft. (9 m)
Yellowish fruits are about 2 in. (5 cm) in diameter and packed with seeds.

Papaya
Carica papaya To 25 ft. (7.6 m)
Branchless tree produces fruit throughout the year. Widely cultivated throughout Hawaii, it was introduced from the American tropics.

Pineapple
Ananas comosus To 2 ft. (60 cm)
The fruit grows in a nest of prickly leaves. An important commercial crop. Native to Brazil.

Sugarcane
Saccharum officinarum
To 20 ft. (6 m)
Tassel-like flower spike blooms late in the year.

INTRODUCED FOOD PLANTS

Banana
Musa spp. To 30 ft. (9 m)
Not a tree, but a tall herb with a stalk made up of tightly clasped leaves. Large leaves (to 12 ft./3.6 m long) are paddle-shaped and tear easily in the wind. Early Hawaiians cultivated over 70 varieties.

Taro
Colocasia esculenta
To 2 ft. (60 cm)
Leaves are heart-shaped. Grows in wet and dry habitats and has been a principal source of food for Hawaiians for hundreds of years. The entire plant is edible.

FERNS, ETC.

Swordfern
Nephrolepis spp.
To 5 ft. (1.5 m)
Fern fronds tend to droop at the end giving this species the local name "fishtail fern." Common along forest trails.

Tree Fern
Cibotium glaucum
To 20 ft. (6 m)
Fronds grow palm-like from the top of a trunk. Stalks are hairy at the base. Common in wet forests.

Bamboo
Schizostachyum glaucifolium
To 35 ft. (10.5 m)
Giant grass forms dense thickets on moist slopes and streambanks. Stems are up to 4 in. (10 cm) in diameter.

False Staghorn Fern
Dicranopteris emarginata
Stems to 15 ft. (4.5 m) long. The common forest fern, it can form dense tangles that are impenetrable.

Lace Fern
Sphenomeris chusana
To 3 ft. (90 cm)
Easily distinguished by its triangular lacy fronds. One of the most common ferns in wet forests throughout Hawaii.

Sadleria Fern
Sadleria cyatheoides
To 5 ft. (1.5 m)
Easily distinguished by its young red fronds that turn green when they mature. Grows only in Hawaii.

Silversword
Argyroxiphium sandwicense
Flower stalk to 10 ft. (3 m)
One of the best-known native Hawaiian plants. Yucca-like plant has stiff, silvery leaves. When the plant matures in 7–30 years, it sends up a flowering spike and dies shortly thereafter. Found in alpine deserts above 6,000 ft. (1800 m).

INTRODUCED ORNAMENTAL PALMS

Royal Palm
Roystonea spp.
To 130 ft. (40 m)
Top of trunk is green and smooth.

Date Palm
Phoenix dactylifera To 75 ft. (23 m)
Has a stout trunk of ascending leaves. Fruits grow in large clusters.

Manila Palm
Veitchia merrillii
To 20 ft. (6 m)
Also called Christmas palm, its bright red fruits ripen Dec.–Jan.

Fan Palm
Washingtonia spp.
To 60 ft. (18 m)
Shaggy sack of dead leaves hangs beneath the crown.

Bottle Palm
Mascarena lagenicaulis
To 20 ft. (6 m)

Canary Palm
Phoenix canariensis To 50 ft. (15 m)
Straight trunk supports crown of enormous leaves up to 23 ft. (7 m) long.

WILDFLOWERS

Night-blooming Cereus
Hylocereus undatus
Vine to 60 ft. (18 m)
Huge flowers bloom in the early evening and wither the next morning between June–October. Native to Mexico.

Common Evening Primrose
Oenothera spp.
To 5 ft. (1.5 m)
Lemon-scented, 4-petalled flowers bloom in the evening.

Bridal Bouquet
Stephanotis floribunda
To 20 ft. (6 m)
Climbing vine has thick leaves and dense flower clusters. Native to Madagascar.

Prickly Pear Cactus
Opuntia spp.
Pads to 12 in. (30 cm)
Prickly pads grow in dense clusters.

Orange Trumpet Vine
Pyrostegia ignea
Climbing vine has brilliant orange flowers that bloom in profusion from January until April. Native to Brazil.

White Ginger
Hedychium coronarium
To 7 ft. (2.1 m)
Flower petals are shaped like a moth. Very fragrant.

WILDFLOWERS

Morning Glory
Ipomoea spp.
Stems to 10 ft. (3 m) long. Creeping plant is the common beach vine. Pink to purple funnel-shaped flowers open in the morning and close later in the day.

Queen Emma Lily
Crinum augustum
To 2 ft. (60 cm)
A favorite of beloved Queen Emma. Native to Mauritius.

Cup of Gold
Solandra maxima
Climbing vine has huge, goblet-shaped flowers up to 9 in. (23 cm) wide. Native to Mexico.

Kahili Ginger
Hedychium gardnerianum
To 8 ft. (2.4 m)
Yellow flowers with bright orange stamens bloom in long terminal spikes. Native to Himalaya.

Passionflower
Passiflora spp.
Climbing vine to 20 ft. (6 m) high. Flowers have a fringe of "tentacles." Native to tropical America.

Turk's Cap
Malvaviscus arboreus
To 5 ft. (1.5 m)
Drooping scarlet flowers have protruding stamens. Native to tropical America.

Spanish Moss
Tillandsia usneoides
To 18 in. (45 cm)
Air plant grows hanging downward from tree branches. Introduced to Hawaii in the 1800s from tropical America, it is a popular ornamental.

Wooden Rose
Merremia tuberosa
Climbing vine
Yellow tubular flowers are succeeded by dried seed pods that look like they've been carved out of satiny, brown wood. Native to tropical America.

Prickly Poppy
Argemone glauca
White flower has tissue-thin petals and a bristle of yellow stamens. Yellow variants also exist.

Shampoo Ginger
Zingiber zerumbet
To 2 ft. (60 cm)
Inconspicuous flowers bloom between scaly red bracts. Mature flower heads secrete a substance Hawaiians used for shampoo. Found in damp, lower forests.

Poinsettia
Euphorbia pulcherrima
To 12 ft. (3.6 m)
Scarlet plant blooms from November to March. White and pink forms also occur. Native to Mexico.

WILDFLOWERS

Anthurium
Anthurium andreaeanum
To 2 ft. (60 cm)
White anthurium (*A. xferrierense*) is also found here. Native to tropical America.

Ti
Cordyline fruticosa
To 10 ft. (3 m)
Shiny leaves are up to 30 in. (75 cm) long. A widely planted ornamental.

Lantana
Lantana camara
To 40 in. (1 m)
Shrub has flowers arranged in an outer and inner ring. Invasive.

Sensitive Plant
Mimosa pudica
To 5 ft. (1.5 m)
Leaves close up when touched and also close at night. Flowers are puffy lavender balls. Native to South America.

Firecracker Plant
Russelia equisetiformis
To 4 ft. (1.2 m)
Droopy shrub has bright red, tubular flowers (to 1 in./3 cm) that bloom throughout the year. Native to Mexico.

Bougainvillea
Bougainvillea spp.
To 30 ft. (9 m)
Thorny shrub features masses of bright red, orange or purple, papery bracts that surround the flowers. Native to Brazil.

Ilima
Sida fallax To 6 ft. (1.8 m)
Yellow-orange flowers (to 1 in./3 cm) resemble miniature hibiscus flowers. Often used in leis.

Pink & Green Heliconia
Heliconia elongata
To 15 ft. (4.5 m)
Native to South America.

Torch Ginger
Phaeomeria magnifica
To 20 ft. (6 m)

Hibiscus
Hibiscus spp. To 33 ft. (10 m)
A tree, shrub or herb distinguished by its unique blossoms with elongate stamens. Comes in a variety of colors. The yellow hibiscus (*Hibiscus brackenridgei*) is **Hawaii's state flower**.

Lobster Claw
Heliconia humilis
To 20 ft. (6 m)
Named for its large red bracts (to 5 in./13 cm long) that resemble broiled lobster claws. Native to South America.

WILDFLOWERS

Bird of Paradise
Strelitzia reginae
To 5 ft. (1.5 m)
Native to South Africa.

Honohono
Commelina spp.
Sprawling herb is found in shady valleys. Flowers have two large blue petals above a tiny white one.

Ko'oko'olau
Bidens spp.
To 4 ft. (1.2 m)
Miniature sunflowers have a button-like central disk and are 1–2 in. (3–5 cm) wide.

Crown Flower
Calotropis gigantea
To 12 ft. (3.6 m)
Shrub has sweet-smelling flowers that have petals rolled back to reveal a miniature ivory crown. Native to India.

Water Hyacinth
Eichhornia crassipes
To 16 in. (40 cm)
Aquatic plant is supported by inflated stalks.

Spider Lily
Hymenocallis spp.
To 30 in. (75 cm)

Spathiphyllum
Spathiphyllum spp.
To 3 ft. (90 cm)
Native to tropical America.

Amaryllis
Hippeastrum spp.
To 20 in. (50 cm)
Over 70 types of amaryllis are cultivated throughout Hawaii. Native to the American tropics.

Traveler's Palm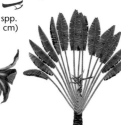
Ravenala madagascariensis
To 30 ft. (9 m)
Although tree-like, it is related to the bird of paradise. Feathery flowers bloom from beak-like cases.

Chinese Ground Orchid
Phaius tankervilleae
To 3 ft. (90 cm)
Striking yellowish flowers have a purplish throat. Native to the South Pacific.

Vanda Miss Joaquim
Vanda teres x hookeriana
To 6 ft. (1.8 m)
One of the most common lei flowers, this hybrid orchid is widely cultivated.

Hawaii Jewel Orchid
Anoectochilus sandvicensis
To 20 in. (50 cm)
Grows in shady, wet areas.